This edition of Spring and All *reproduces
the original 1923 edition,
published by Contact Press,
with a new introduction by C. D. Wright.*

T0367099

BY WILLIAM CARLOS WILLIAMS
from New Directions

Spring and All

by

William Carlos Williams

Introduction by C. D. Wright

A NEW DIRECTIONS BOOK

New Directions would like to thank the New York Public Library for their assistance in the production of this book.

Manufactured in the United States of America
First published as a New Directions Paperbook Original (NDP1208) in 2011

Library of Congress Cataloging-in-Publication Data
Williams, William Carlos, 1883–1963.
Spring and all / William Carlos Williams.
p. cm.
"A New Directions Pearl."
ISBN 978-0-8112-1891-7 (pbk. : acid-free paper)
I. Title.
PS3545.I544S7 2010
811′.52—dc22   2010021394

10 9 8

New Directions Books are published for James Laughlin
by New Directions Publishing Corporation
80 Eighth Avenue, New York 10011

INTRODUCTION

It is difficult...
to read now
how it was then
yet...

The Great War is barely in the background. The fatal flu pandemic fills the void, concentrating on the young and healthy. This weird little book is brought into the world the same month as the Munich Beer Hall Putsch, Hitler's first major drive to seize control. Among artists and writers, the urge for renewal is gaining ground in the aftermath of monstrous destruction, in the bud of worse to come. It is boggling that so much hearty artistic innovation has commenced to proliferate and thrive. Do or die. Those who can, do. Even the wreckage of Europe is tempting to the young, creative, contrary, and restless. One American writer stays put, finishes school, starts a medical practice. One American writer sticks around to catch the babies.

* * *

1923: Wallace Stevens's *Harmonium* was published, Mina Loy's *Lunar Baedecker*, Jean Toomer's unassimilable hybrid masterwork, *Cane*, and *Spring and All*, an equally unassimilable hybrid masterwork. That year, Yeats, whose dominance in poetry was commonly acknowledged, was awarded the Nobel Prize. Marianne Moore's *Observations* and Gertrude Stein's *The Making of Americans* were soon to clear the horizon. The former would be as steady on its feet as a wading bird; the latter, a bollard of granite. The leonine-haired Ezra Pound was the force upon which many depended and with which all had to contend. Staying on his own side of the Atlantic tendered William Carlos Williams the breathing room he needed.

Spring and All was printed in Dijon, by the same Darantiere who had printed *Ulysses* the year before; so the printer, at least, was already familiar with the oddities the English language could bear. Robert McAlmon's Paris-based Contact Publishing Company issued Williams's manifesto-of-sorts in an edition of three hundred, most of which went undistributed. The year before, 1922, was high tide in poetry: *The Duino Elegies*, *Trilce*, and *The Waste Land*. The latter was a head blow to William Carlos Williams. He had more or less absorbed the concussion of "Prufrock" and sounded off on it in his prologue to *Kora in Hell*. He had already recalibrated and redoubled to the task of staking out the new word for the not-so-new-anymore world. Then came *The Waste Land*, all tricked out with Sanscrit and Latin ornaments. The impact was as useful as it was painful. Whap. Now he knew what he was opposing; now he could move in the direction he wanted to go–forward–in his "small or large machine made of words." For Williams, poetry was meant to be in motion. He willed himself ready: "How easy to slip / into the old mode, how hard to / cling firmly to the advance–"

Williams epitomized the prepared observer. A watcher, a listener. Goat stubborn. Feet-in-the-soil independent. He could write whatever, whenever, and as he damn well pleased. William Carlos Williams was the embodiment of the values Americans touted but seemed capable of expressing only in "isolate flecks." With an English father and Puerto Rican mother, there was no compelling incentive to become an expat. He would embrace the contrary impulse. Like his fellow New Jerseyan, Whitman, his apostrophe was to the future, but he hankered for contact here and now. The charge of this writing was change. His own personal epic and constantly shifting landscape was just on the other side of the parlor window, the whole procession. Like Whitman, he would gradually come to a great human understanding, an apprehension that eluded a number of his peers.

Between great hails to the imagination and salvos of opprobrium, William Carlos Williams set one sharp-edged poem after another into the composition of an unframed original. So the one who did not cast off his roots chose the oldest trope in the book, SPRING, to push and pull American poetry into the present tense. Not before he had initiated a willful number of false starts, cranking up anticipation and repeatedly sabotaging expectations. Not before the hectored reader was fetched up "by the road to the contagious hospital"– only then would the first glimpse of grass and "the stiff curl of the wildcarrot leaf" be permitted– at the precise point at which every stick in

the refuse emerged particular. *Terrifying*, as Robert Cree-
ley was given to say.

From page one, the doctor lurches into an exchange
with his imaginary critics. In lieu of titles or subtitles or
headings, he spoofs the typographical stunts of the times,
using both Arabic and Roman "chapters" to fence off units
of poetry and prose, completely out of sequence. *Chapter
XIII* appears upside down. The effect creates a minor dis-
traction, albeit intentional, but it is the abrupt shifting,
cutting, and swerving that prevent the reader from ever
relaxing into the text. The suspense of the performance
is carried all the way to "the edge of the petal." Does love
wait there? Will spring ever come? Who is Kiki – the nurse,
the French artist model, the waif in the long-running play?
Will the doctor please elucidate what he christens *imagi-
nation*? What does J. P. Morgan have to do with anything
except what new money can buy, Old Masters? What does
it mean to be "drunk with goats or pavement"? Country or
city? Who else but Williams would grasp that the place to
get the latest news about the weather and the last word on
death is the barbershop? Who else cared what the barber
thought? And when the whole atavistic American scene
gets intolerable, would anyone be there to drive the car?
Tranquilly Titicaca indeed.

The prose is a working-through – hot with argument,
loud with opinion. The overall form is a grand improvi-
sation. Here a little rapture on the possible; here a riff on
Shakespeare, on Poe, on Anatole France. The poetry was
struck in one sitting, executed with what Hugh Kenner

called Williams's "great technical perception." Here an ekphrastic poem on a painting by Juan Gris; here an homage to le jazz hot, le jazz cool; here a snapshot of what he saw through the windshield, or notations scribbled into a prescription pad. References ladled out of the "skyscraper soup" of industry, advertising, local speech–all the while spring itself was stiffly becoming manifest.

Yet, for the mash-up of affinities, free-floating associations, and spasms of anger, Williams loved simplicity and order. He avoided the sesquipedalian habits of Pound and Eliot. The stripped-down poems in *Spring & All* are as quick and unencumbered as any nude tripping down the stairs. The choice enjambment, "under the surge of the blue / mottled clouds," the lucent precision of the modest noun *glaze*, and the assertion that "The rose is obsolete" were stock-in-trade. He delivered the language scrubbed clean, made new.

This was a gutsy, self-conscious generation of writers and artists. They all knew each other. Pound and H.D. and the painter, Charles Demuth, to whom this book is dedicated, were friends from the college years. Williams was soon to befriend Wallace Stevens and Marianne Moore and Mina Loy. The Stieglitz crowd. Duchamp and the collector Walter Arensberg, and on and on. They promoted and financed one another's dreams, shared and competed for lovers, for recognition and influence. Williams's profession planted him. In the city, the painters seeded his ideas. And he was there in the first rub, reading his "Overture to a Dance of Locomotives" at the 1913 Armory Show.

(Ms. Loy was impressed, but not enough to lie with him.)

Williams was, according to Pound, the "hardiest speci-men in these parts." While zealously promoting the su-premacy of the imagination, he dealt in real things, with individuals in real and current need. In his line of work, people were literally exposed. Then there was the end-less variety of the species, which suited what Williams re-ferred to as his nervous nature. Then everything along the roadside just popped out and demanded his immedi-ate attention. He was a local. He was "seeking to articu-late," seeking "to name it." He resisted revision. He loved art. He spoke "plain American." He had a thirst for *now*. And he had his own beat, "a certain unquenchable exalta-tion" as he said of his renowned wheelbarrow. The excite-ment the writing exuded is as *contagious* today as when he made his rounds "quickened by the life about him." The reader is induced to stay awake. Make contact. Look ahead. In 1923, poetry's backward advance came to the crossroads. The pediatrician from Rutherford discharged the symbolic heap of myth and metaphor; adjusted his fo-cal length to light up cast-off, common things; dug his heels into American dirt and passed directly into the mo-ment. Ah, SPRING.

– C. D. WRIGHT

SPRING AND ALL

To

Charles Demuth

Spring and All

I F anything of moment results — so much the
   better. And so much the more likely will it be
that no one will want to see it.

There is a constant barrier between the reader
and his consciousness of immediate contact with
the world. If there is an ocean it is here. Or rather,
the whole world is between : Yesterday, tomorrow,
Europe, Asia, Africa, — all things removed and
impossible, the tower of the church at Seville, the
Parthenon.

What do they mean when they say : ,, I do not
like your poems ; you have no faith whatever. You
seem neither to have suffered nor, in fact, to have
felt anything very deeply. There is nothing appealing
in what you say but on the contrary the poems are
positively repellant. They are heartless, cruel, they
make fun of humanity. What in God's name do you
mean ? Are you a pagan ? Have you no tolerance
for human frailty ? Rhyme you may perhaps take

away but rythm ! why there is none in your work whatever. Is this what you call poetry ? It is the very antithesis of poetry. It is antipoetry. It is the annihilation of life upon which you are bent. Poetry that used to go hand in hand with life, poetry that interpreted our deepest promptings, poetry that inspired, that led us forward to new discoveries, new depths of tolerance, new heights of exaltation. You moderns ! it is the death of poetry that you are accomplishing. No. I cannot understand this work. You have not yet suffered a cruel blow from life. When you have suffered you will write differently ? »

Perhaps this noble apostrophy means something terrible for me, I am not certain, but for the moment I interpret it to say : « You have robbed me. God, I am naked. What shall I do ? » — By it they mean that when I have suffered (provided I have not done so as yet) I too shall run for cover ; that I too shall seek refuge in fantasy. And mind you, I do not say that I will not. To decorate my age.

But today it is different.

The reader knows himself as he was twenty years ago and he has also in mind a vision of what he would be, some day. Oh, some day ! But the thing he never knows and never dares to know is what he is at the exact moment that he is. And this moment is the only thing in which I am at all interested. Ergo, who cares for anything I do ? And what do I care ?

I love my fellow creature. Jesus, how I love him : endways, sideways, frontways and all the other ways — but he doesn't exist ! Neither does she. I do, in a bastardly sort of way.

To whom then am I addressed ? To the imagination.

In fact to return upon my theme for the time nearly all writing, up to the present, if not all art, has been especially designed to keep up the barrier between sense and the vaporous fringe which distracts the attention from its agonized approaches to the moment. It has been always a search for ,, the beautiful illusion ''. Very well. I am not in search of ,, the beautiful illusion ''.

And if when I pompously announce that I am addressed — To the imagination — you believe that I thus divorce myself from life and so defeat my own end, I reply : To refine, to clarify, to intensify that eternal moment in which we alone live there is but a single force — the imagination. This is its book. I myself invite you to read and to see.

In the imagination, we are from henceforth (so

long as you read) locked in a fraternal embrace, the classic caress of author and reader. We are one. Whenever I say ,, I '' I mean also ,, you ''. And so, together, as one, we shall begin.

CHAPTER 19

o meager times, so fat in everything imaginable ! imagine the New World that rises to our windows from the sea on Mondays and on Saturdays — and on every other day of the week also. Imagine it in all its prismatic colorings, its counterpart in our souls — our souls that are great pianos whose strings, of honey and of steel, the divisions of the rainbow set twanging, loosing on the air great novels of adventure ! Imagine the monster project of the moment : Tomorrow we the people of the United States are going to Europe armed to kill every man, woman and child in the area west of the Carpathian Mountains (also east) sparing none. Imagine the sensation it will cause. First we shall kill them and then they, us. But we are careful to spare the Spanish bulls, the birds, rabbits, small deer and of course — the Russians. For the Russians we shall build a bridge from edge to edge of the Atlantic — having first been at pains to slaughter all Canadians and Mexicans on this side. Then, oh then, the great feature will take place.

Never mind ; the great event may not exist, so there is no need to speak further of it. Kill ! kill ! the English, the Irish, the French, the Germans, the Italians and the rest : friends or enemies, it makes no difference, kill them all. The bridge is to be blown up when all Russia is upon it. And why ?

Because we love them — all. That is the secret : a new sort of murder. We make leberwurst of them. Bratwurst. But why, since we are ourselves doomed to suffer the same annihilation ?

If I could say what is in my mind in Sanscrit or even Latin I would do so. But I cannot. I speak for the integrity of the soul and the greatness of life's inanity ; the formality of its boredom ; the orthodoxy of its stupidity. Kill ! kill ! let there be fresh meat...

The imagination, intoxicated by prohibitions, rises to drunken heights to destroy the world. Let it rage, let it kill. The imagination is supreme. To it all our works forever, from the remotest past to the farthest future, have been, are and will be dedicated. To it alone we show our wit by having raised in its honor as monument not the least pebble. To it now we come to dedicate our secret project : the annihilation of every human creature on the face of the earth. This is something never before attempted. None to remain ; nothing but the lower vertebrates, the mollusks, insects and plants. Then at last will the world be made anew. Houses crumble to ruin, cities disappear giving place to mounds of soil blown thither by the winds, small bushes and grass give way to trees which grow old and are succeeded by other trees for countless generations. A marvellous serenity broken only by bird and wild beast calls reigns over the entire sphere. Order and peace abound.

This final and self inflicted holocaust has been all for love, for sweetest love, that together the human race, yellow, black, brown, red and white, agglutinated into one enormous soul may be gratified with the sight and retire to the heaven of heavens content to rest on its laurels. There, soul of souls, watching its own horrid unity, it boils and digests itself within the tissues of the great Being of Eternity that we shall then have become. With what magnificent explosions and odors will not the day be accomplished as we, the Great One among all creatures, shall go about contemplating our self-prohibited desires as we promenade them before the inward review of our own bowels — et cetera, et cetera, et cetera... and it is spring — both in Latin and Turkish, in English and Dutch, in Japanese and Italian ; it is spring by Stinking River where a magnolia tree, without leaves, before what was once a farmhouse, now a ramshackle home for millworkers, raises its straggling branches of ivorywhite flowers.

CHAPTER XIII

Thus, weary of life, in view of the great consummation which awaits us — tomorrow, we rush among our friends congratulating ourselves upon the joy soon to be. Thoughtless of evil we crush out the marrow of those about us with our heavy cars as we go happily from place to place. It seems that there is not time enough in which to speak the full of our exaltation. Only a day is left, one miserable day, before the world comes into its own. Let us hurry ! Why bother for this man or that ? In the offices of the great newspapers a mad joy reigns as they prepare the final extras. Rushing about, men bump each other into the whirring presses. How funny it seems. All thought of misery has left us. Why should we care ? Children laughingly fling themselves under the wheels of the street cars, airplanes crash gaily to the earth. Someone has written a poem.

Oh life, bizarre fowl, what color are your wings ? Green, blue, red, yellow, purple, white, brown, orange, black, grey ? In the imagination, flying above the wreck of ten thousand million souls, I see you departing sadly for the land of plants and insects, already far out to sea. (Thank you, I know well what

I am plagiarising) Your great wings flap as you disappear in the distance over the pre-Columbian acres of floating weed.

The new cathedral overlooking the park, looked down from its towers today, with great eyes, and saw by the decorative lake a group of people staring curiously at the corpse of a suicide : Peaceful, dead young man, the money they have put into the stones has been spent to teach men of life's austerity. You died and teach us the same lesson. You seem a cathedral, celebrant of the spring which shivers for me among the long black trees.

CHAPTER VI

Now, in the imagination, all flesh, all human flesh has been dead upon the earth for ten million, billion years. The bird has turned into a stone within whose heart an egg, unlayed, remained hidden.

It is spring ! but miracle of miracles a miraculous miracle has gradually taken place during these seemingly wasted eons. Through the orderly sequences of unmentionable time EVOLUTION HAS REPEATED ITSELF FROM THE BEGINNING.

Good God !

Every step once taken in the first advance of the human race, from the amoeba to the highest type of intelligence, has been duplicated, every step exactly paralleling the one that preceeded in the dead ages gone by. A perfect plagiarism results· Everything is and is new. Only the imagination is undeceived.

At this point the entire complicated and laborious process begins to near a new day. (More of this in Chapter XIX) But for the moment everything is fresh, perfect, recreated.

In fact now, for the first time, everything IS new. Now at last the perfect effect is being witlessly discovered. The terms ,, veracity " ,, actuality " ,, real " ,, natural " ,, sincere " are being discussed at length, every word in the discussion being evolved from an identical discussion which took place the day before yesterday.

Yes, the imagination, drunk with prohibitions, has destroyed and recreated everything afresh in the likeness of that which it was. Now indeed men look about in amazement at each other with a full realization of the meaning of ,, art ".

CHAPTER 2

It is spring : life again begins to assume its normal appearence as of ,, today ''. Only the imagination is undeceived. The volcanos are extinct. Coal is beginning to be dug again where the fern forests stood last night. (If an error is noted here, pay no attention to it).

CHAPTER XIX

I realize that the chapters are rather quick in their sequence and that nothing much is contained in any one of them but no one should be surprised at this today.

THE TRADITIONALISTS OF PLAGIARISM

It is spring. That is to say, it is approaching THE BEGINNING.

In that huge and microscopic career of time, as it were a wild horse racing in an illimitable pampa under the stars, describing immense and microscopic circles with his hoofs on the solid turf, running without a stop for the millionth part of a second until he is aged and worn to a heap of skin, bones and ragged hoofs — In that majestic progress of life, that gives the exact impression of Phidias' frizze, the men and beasts of which, though they seem of the rigidity of marble are not so but move, with blinding rapidity, though we do not have the time to notice it, their legs advancing a millionth part of an inch every fifty thousand years — In that progress of life which seems stillness itself in the mass of its movements — at last SPRING is approaching.

In that colossal surge toward the finite and the capable life has now arrived for the second time at that exact moment when in the ages past the destruction of the species *Homo sapiens* occured.

Now at last that process of miraculous verisimilitude, that grate copying which evolution has followed, repeating move for move every move that it made in the past — is approaching the end.

Suddenly it is at an end. THE WORLD IS NEW.

I

By the road to the contagious hospital
under the surge of the blue
mottled clouds driven from the

northeast — a cold wind. Beyond, the
waste of broad, muddy fields
brown with dried weeds, standing and fallen

patches of standing water
the scattering of tall trees

All along the road the reddish
purplish, forked, upstanding, twiggy
stuff of bushes and small trees
with dead, brown leaves under them
leafless vines —

Lifeless in appearance, sluggish
dazed spring approaches —

They enter the new world naked,
cold, uncertain of all
save that they enter. All about them
the cold, familiar wind —

Now the grass, tomorrow
the stiff curl of wildcarrot leaf

One by one objects are defined —
It quickens : clarity, outline of leaf

But now the stark dignity of
entrance — Still, the profound change

has come upon then : rooted they
grip down and begin to awaken

II

Pink confused with white
flowers and flowers reversed
take and spill the shaded flame
darting it back
into the lamp's horn

petals aslant darkened with mauve

red where in whorls
petal lays its glow upon petal
round flamegreen throats

petals radiant with transpiercing light
contending
                              above

the leaves
reaching up their modest green
from the pot's rim

and there, wholly dark, the pot
gay with rough moss.

A terrific confusion has taken place. No man knows whither to turn. There is nothing ! Emptiness stares us once more in the face. Whither ? To what end ? Each asks the other. Has life its tail in its mouth or its mouth in its tail ? Why are we here ? Dora Marsden's philosophic algebra. Everywhere men look into each other's faces and ask the old unanswerable question : Whither ? How ? What ? Why ?

At any rate, now at last spring is here !

The rock has split, the egg has hatched, the prismatically plumed bird of life has escaped from its cage. It spreads its wings and is perched now on the peak of the huge African mountain Kilimanjaro.

Strange recompense, in the depths of our despair at the unfathomable mist into which all mankind is plunging, a curious force awakens. It is HOPE long asleep, aroused once more. Wilson has taken an army of advisers and sailed for England. The ship has sunk. But the men are all good swimmers. They take the women on their shoulders and buoyed on by the inspiration of the moment they churn the free seas with their sinewey arms, like Ulysses, landing all along the European seaboard.

Yes, hope has awakened once more in men's hearts. It is the NEW ! Let us go forward !

The imagination, freed from the handcuffs of „ art ", takes the lead ! Her feet are bare and not too delicate. In fact those who come behind her have much to think of. Hm. Let it pass.

CHAPTER I

SAMUEL BUTLER

The great English divine, Sam Butler, is shouting from a platform, warning us as we pass : There are two who can invent some extraordinary thing to one who can properly employ that which has been made use of before.

Enheartened by this thought THE TRADI-TIONALISTS OF PLAGIARISM try to get hold of the mob. They seize those nearest them and shout into their ears : Tradition ! The solidarity of life !

The fight is on : These men who have had the governing of the mob through all the repetitious years resent the new order. Who can answer them ? One perhaps here and there but it is an impossible situation. If life were anything but a bird, if it were a man, a Greek or an Egyptian, but it is only a bird that has eyes and wings, a beak, talons and a cry that reaches to every rock's center, but without intelligence ? —

The voice of the Delphic Oracle itself, what was it ? A poisonous gas from a rock's cleft.

Those who led yesterday wish to hold their sway a while longer. It is not difficult to understand their mood. They have their great weapons to hand : ,, science ", ,, philosophy " and most dangerous of all ,, art ".

Meanwhile, SPRING, which has been approaching for several pages, is at last here.

— they ask us to return to the proven truths of tradition, even to the twice proven, the substantiality of which is known. Demuth and a few others do their best to point out the error, telling us that design is a function of the IMAGINATION, describing its movements, its colors — but it is a hard battle. I myself seek to enter the lists with these few notes jotted down in the midst of the action, under distracting circumstances — to remind myself (see p. 2, paragraph 4) of the truth.

III

The farmer in deep thought
is pacing through the rain
among his blank fields, with
hands in pockets,

in his head
the harvest already planted.
A cold wind ruffles the water
among the browned weeds.
On all sides
the world rolls coldly away :
black orchards
darkened by the March clouds —
leaving room for thought.
Down past the brushwood
bristling by
the rainsluiced wagonroad
looms the artist figure of
the farmer — composing
— antagonist

                    IV

The Easter stars are shining
above lights that are flashing —
coronal of the black —
                        Nobody
to say it —
            Nobody to say : pinholes

Thither I would carry her
among the lights —
Burst it asunder

break through to the fifty words
necessary —-

       a crown for her head with
castles upon it, skyscrapers
filled with nut-chocolates —

       dovetame winds —
stars of tinsel
from the great end of a cornucopia
of glass

So long as the sky is recognised as an association

is recognised in its function of accessory to vague words whose meaning it is impossible to rediscover its value can be nothing but mathematical certain limits of gravity and density of air

The farmer and the fisherman who read their own lives there have a practical corrective for —

they rediscover or replace demoded meanings to the religious terms

Among them, without expansion of imagination, there is the residual contact between life and the imagination which is essential to freedom

The man of imagination who turns to art for release and fulfilment of his baby promises contends with the sky through layers of demoded words and shapes. Demoded, not because the essential vitality which begot them is laid waste — this cannot be so, a young man feels, since he feels it in himself

— but because meanings have been lost through laziness or changes in the form of existance which have let words empty.

Bare handed the man contends with the sky, without experience of existence seeking to invent and design.

Crude symbolism is to associate emotions with natural phenomena such as anger with lightning, flowers with love it goes further and associates certain textures with

Such work is empty. It is very typical of almost all that is done by the writers who fill the pages every month of such a paper as. Everything that I have done in the past — except those parts which may be called excellent — by chance, have that quality about them.

It is typified by use of the word « like » or that « evocation » of the « image » which served us for a time. Its abuse is apparent. The insignificant « image » may be « evoked » never so ably and still mean nothing.

With all his faults Alfred Kreymborg never did this. That is why his work — escaping a common fault — still has value and will tomorrow have more.

Sandburg, when uninspired by intimacies of the eye and ear, runs into this empty symbolism. Such poets of promise as ruin themselves with it, though many have major sentimental faults besides.

Marianne Moore escapes. The incomprehensibility of her poems is witness to at what cost (she cleaves herself away) as it is also to the distance which the most are from a comprehension of the purpose of composition.

The better work men do is always done under stress and at great personal cost.

It is no different from the aristocratic compositions of the earlier times, The Homeric inventions

but
these occured in different times, to this extent, that life had not yed sieved through its own multiformity. That aside, the work the two-thousand-year-old poet did and that we do are one piece. That is the vitality of the classics.

So then — Nothing is put down in the present book —-except through weakness of the imagination — which is not intended as of a piece with the « nature » which Shakespeare mentions and which Hartley

speaks of so completely in his « Adventures » : it is
the common thing which is annonymously about us.

Composition is in no essential an escape from life.
In fact if it is so it is negligeable to the point of insig-
nificance. Whatever « life » the artist may be forced
to lead has no relation to the vitality of his compo-
sitions. Such names as Homer, the blind ; Schehe-
razade, who lived under threat — Their compositions
have as their excellence an identity with life since
they are as actual, as sappy as the leaf of the tree
which never moves from one spot.

What I put down of value will have this value :
an escape from crude symbolism, the annihilation
of strained associations, complicated ritualistic forms
designed to separate the work from « reality » — such
as rhyme, meter as meter and not as the essential of
the work, one of its words.

But this smacks too much of the nature of — This
is all negative and appears to be boastful. It is not
intended to be so. Rather the opposite

The work will be in the realm of the imagination
as plain as the sky is to a fisherman — A very clouded
sentence. The word must be put down for itself, not
as a symbol of nature but a part, cognisant of the
whole — aware — civilized.

V

Blacks wind from the north
enter black hearts. Barred from
seclusion in lilys they strike
to destroy —

Beastly humanity
where the wind breaks it —

                              strident voices, heat
quickened, built of waves

Drunk with goats or pavements

Hate his of the night and the day
of flowers and rocks. Nothing
is gained by saying the night breeds
murder — It is the classical mistake

The day

All that enters in another person
all grass, all blackbirds flying
all azalia trees in flower
salt winds —

Sold to them men knock blindly together
splitting their heads open

That is why boxing matches and
Chinese poems are the same — That is why
Hartley praises Miss Wirt

There is nothing in the twist
of the wind but — dashes of cold rain

It is one with submarine vistas
purple and black fish turning
among undulant seaweed —

Black wind, I have poured my heart out
to you until I am sick of it —-

Now I run my hand over you feeling
the play of your body — the quiver
of its strength —

The grief of the bowmen of Shu
moves nearer — There is
an approach with difficulty from
the dead — the winter casing of grief

How easy to slip
into the old mode, how hard to
cling firmly to the advance —

VI

No that is not it
nothing that I have done
nothing
I have done

is made up of
nothing
and the dipthong

ae

together with
the first person
singular
indicative

of the auxilliary
verb
to have

everything
I have done
is the same

if to do

is capable
of an
infinity of
combinations

involving the
moral
physical
and religious

codes

for everything
and nothing
are synonymous
when '

energy in vacuuo
has the power
of confusion

which only to
have done nothing
can make
perfect

    The inevitable flux of the seeing eye toward meas-
uring itself by the world it inhabits can only result

in himself crushing humiliation unless the individual raise to some approximate co-extension with the universe. This is possible by aid of the imagination. Only through the agency of this force can a man feel himself moved largely with sympathetic pulses at work —

A work of the imagination which fails to release the senses in accordance with this major requisite — the sympathies, the intelligence in its selective world, fails at the elucidation, the alleviation which is —

In the composition, the artist does exactly what every eye must do with life, fix the particular with the universality of his own personality — Taught by the largeness of his imagination to feel every form which he sees moving within himself, he must prove the truth of this by expression.

The contraction which is felt.

All this being anterior to technique, that can have only a sequent value ; but since all that appears to the senses on a work of art does so through
                                        fixation by
the imagination of the external as well internal means of expression the essential nature of technique or transcription.

Only when this position is reached can life proper

be said to begin since only then can a value be affixed to the forms and activities of which it consists.

Only then can the sense of frustration which ends. All composition defeated.

Only through the imagination is the advance of intelligence possible, to keep beside growing understanding.

Complete lack of imagination would be the same at the cost of intelligence, complete.

Even the most robust constitution has its limits, though the Roman feast with its reliance upon regurgitation to prolong it shows an active ingenuity, yet the powers of a man are so pitifully small, with the ocean to swallow — that at the end of the feast nothing would be left but suicide.

That or the imagination which in this case takes the form of humor, is known in that form — the release from physical necessity. Having eaten to the full we must acknowledge our insufficiency since we have not annihilated all food nor even the quantity of a good sized steer. However we have annihilated all eating : quite plainly we have no more appetite. This is to say that the imagination has removed us from the banal necessity of bursting ourselves — by

acknowledging a new situation. We must acknowledge
that the ocean we would drink is too vast — but at
the same time we realize that extension in our case
is not confined to the intestine only. The stomach
is full, the ocean no fuller, both have the same qua-
lity of fullness. In that, then, one is equal to the
other. Having eaten, the man has released his mind.

THIS catalogue might be increased to larger pro-
portions without stimulating the sense.

In works of the imagination that which is taken
for great good sense, so that it seems as if an accurate
precept were discovered, is in reality not so, but
vigor and accuracy of the imagination alone. In work
such as Shakespeares —

This leads to the discovery that has been made
today — old catalogues aside — full of meat —

" the divine illusion has about it that inaccuracy
which reveals that which I mean ".

There is only ,, illusion " in art where ignorance
of the bystander confuses imagination and its works
with cruder processes. Truly men feel an enlarge-
ment before great or good work, an expansion but
this is not, as so many believe today a ,, lie ", a
stupefaction, a kind of mesmerism, a thing to block

out " life ", bitter to the individual, by a " vision of beauty ". It is a work of the imagination. It gives the feeling of completion by revealing the oneness of experience ; it rouses rather than stupefies the intelligence by demonstrating the importance of personality, by showing the individual, depressed before it, that his life is valuable — when completed by the imagination. And then only. Such work elucidates —

Such a realization shows us the falseness of attempting to " copy " nature. The thing is equally silly when we try to " make " pictures —

But such a picture as that of Juan Gris, though I have not seen it in color, is important as marking more clearly than any I have seen what the modern trend is : the attempt is being made to separate things of the imagination from life, and obviously, by using the forms common to experience so as not to frighten the onlooker away but to invite him,

> The rose is obsolete
> but each petal ends in
> an edge, the double facet
> cementing the grooved
> columns of air — The edge
> cuts without cutting

meets — nothing — renews
itself in metal or porcelain —

whither ? It ends —

But if it ends
the start is begun
so that to engage roses
becomes a geometry —

Sharper, neater, more cutting
figured in majolica —
the broken plate
glazed with a rose

Somewhere the sense
makes copper roses
steel roses —

The rose carried weight of love
but love is at an end — of roses

If is at the edge of the
petal that love waits

Crisp, worked to defeat
laboredness — fragile
plucked, moist, half-raised
cold, precise, touching

What

The place between the petal's
edge and the

From the petal's edge a line starts
that being of steel
infinitely fine, infinitely
rigid penetrates
the Milky Way
without contact — lifting
from it — neither hanging
nor pushing —

The fragility of the flower
unbruised
penetrates spaces

VIII

The sunlight in a
yellow plaque upon the
varnished floor

is full of a song
inflated to
fifty pounds pressure

at the faucet of
June that rings
the triangle of the air

pulling at the
anemonies in
Persephone's cow pasture —

When from among
the steel rocks leaps
J. P. M.

who enjoyed
extraordinary privileges
among virginity

to solve the core
of whirling flywheels
by cutting

the Gordian knot
with a Veronese or
perhaps a Rubens —

whose cars are about
the finest on
the market today —

And so it comes

to motor cars —
which is the son

leaving off the g
of sunlight and grass —
Impossible

to say, impossible
to underestimate —
wind, earthquakes in

Manchuria, a
partridge
from dry leaves

    things with which he is familiar, simple things
— at the same time to detach them from ordinary
experience to the imagination. Thus they are still
" real " they are the same things they would be
it photographed or painted by Monet, they are
recognizable as the things touched by the hands
during the day, but in this painting they are seen
to be in some peculiar way — detached

Here is a shutter, a bunch of grapes, a sheet of
music, a picture of sea and mountains (particularly
fine) which the onlooker is not for a moment permitted
to witness as an " illusion ". One thing laps over
on the other, the cloud laps over on the shutter,

the bunch of grapes is part of the handle of the
guitar, the mountain and sea are obviously not
" the mountain and sea ", but a picture of the
mountain and the sea. All drawn with admirable
simplicity and excellent design —· all a unity —

This was not necessary where the subject of art
was not " reality " but related to the " gods " —
by force or otherwise. There was no need of the
" illusion " in such a case since there was none
possible where a picture or a work represented
simply the imaginative reality which existed in the
mind of the onlooker. No special effort was necessary
to cleave where the cleavage already existed.

I don't know what the Spanish see in their Velas-
quez and Goya but

Today where everything is being brought into
sight the realism of art has bewildered us, confused
us and forced us to re-invent in order to retain
that which the older generations had without that
effort.

Cezanne —

The only realism in art is of the imagination.
It is only thus that the work escapes plagiarism
after nature and becomes a creation

Invention of new forms to embody this reality
of art, the one thing which art is, must occupy all
serious minds concerned.

From the time of Poe in the U. S. — the first
American poet had to be a man of great separation —
with close identity with life. Poe could not have
written a word without the violence of expulsive
emotion combined with the in-driving force of a
crudely repressive environment. Between the two
his imagination was forced into being to keep him
to that reality, completeness, sense of escape which
is felt in his work — his topics. Typically American
— accurately, even inevitably set in his time.

So, after this tedious diversion —- whatever of
dull you find among my work, put it down to criti-
cism, not to poetry. You will not be mistaken —
Who am I but my own critic ? Surely in isolation
one becomes a god — At least one becomes something
of everything, which is not wholly godlike, yet a
little so — in many things.

It is not necessary to count every flake of the
truth that falls ; it is necessary to dwell in the
imagination if the truth is to be numbered. It is
necessary to speak from the imagination —

The great furor about perspective in Holbein's

day had as a consequence much fine drawing, it made coins defy gravity, standing on the table as if in the act of falling. To say this was lifelike must have been satisfying to the master, it gave depth, pungency.

But all the while the picture escaped notice — partly because of the perspective. Or if noticed it was for the most part because one could see " the birds pecking at the grapes " in it.

Meanwhile the birds were pecking at the grapes outside the window and in the next street Bauermeister Kummel was letting a gold coin slip from his fingers to the counting table.

The representation was perfect, it " said something one was used to hearing " but with verve, cleverly.

Thus perspective and clever drawing kept the picture continually under cover of the " beautiful illusion " until today, when even Anatole France trips, saying : " Art — all lies ! " — today when we are beginning to discover the truth that in great works of the imagination A CREATIVE FORCE IS SHOWN AT WORK MAKING OBJECTS WHICH ALONE COMPLETE SCIENCE AND ALLOW INTELLIGENCE TO SURVIVE — his picture lives anew. It lives as pictures only can : by their power TO ESCAPE ILLUSION and stand between man and nature as saints once stood between man and the sky — their reality in such work, say, as that of Juan Gris

No man could suffer the fragmentary nature of his understanding of his own life —

Whitman's proposals are of the same piece with the modern trend toward imaginative understanding of life. The largeness which he interprets as his identity with the least and the greatest about him, his " demo-cracy " represents the vigor of his imaginative life.

IX

What about all this writing ?

O " Kiki "
O Miss Margaret Jarvis
The backhandspring

I : clean
    clean
    clean : yes.. New-York

Wrigley's, appendecitis, John Marin :
skyscraper soup —

Either that or a bullet !

Once
anything might have happened
You lay relaxed on my knees —
the starry night
spread out warm and blind
above the hospital —

Pah !

It is unclean
which is not straight to the mark —

In my life the furniture eats me

the chairs, the floor
the walls
which heard your sobs
drank up my emotion —
they which alone know everything

and snitched on us in the morning —

What to want ?

Drunk we go forward surely
Not I

beds, beds, beds
elevators, fruit, night-tables
breasts to see, white and blue —
to hold in the hand, to nozzle

It is not onion soup
Your sobs soaked through the walls
breaking the hospital to pieces

Everything
— windows, chairs
obscenely drunk, spinning —
white ,blue, orange
— hot with our passion

wild tears, desperate rejoinders
my legs, turning slowly
end over end in the air !

But what would you have ?

All I said was :
there, you see, it is broken

stockings, shoes, hairpins
your bed, I wrapped myself round you —

I watched.

You sobbed, you beat your pillow
you tore your hair
you dug your nails into your sides

I was your nightgown
                      I   watched !

Clean is he alone
after whom stream
the broken pieces of the city —
flying apart at his approaches

but I merely
caress you curiously

fifteen years ago and you still
go about the city, they say
patching up sick school children

    Understood in a practical way, without calling
upon mystic agencies, of this or that order, it is that
life becomes actual only when it is identified with
ourselves. When we name it, life exists. To repeat
physical experiences has no —

    The only means he has to give value to life is to
recognise it with the imagination and name it ; this is

so. To repeat and repeat the thing without naming it is only to dull the sense and results in frustration.

this make the artist the prey of life. He is easy of attack.

I think often of my earlier work and what it has cost me not to have been clear. I acknowledge I have moved chaotically about refusing or rejecting most things, seldom accepting values or acknowledging anything.

because I early recognised the futility of acquisitive understanding and at the same time rejected religious dogmatism. My whole life has been spent (so far) in seeking to place a value upon experience and the objects of experience that would satisfy my sense of inclusiveness without redundancy — completeness, lack of frustration with the liberty of choice ; the things which the pursuit of « art » offers —

But though I have felt « free » only in the presence of works of the imagination, knowing the quickening of the sense which came of it, and though this experience has held me firm at such times, yet being of a slow but accurate understanding, I have not always been able to complete the intellectual steps which would make me firm in the position.

So most of my life has been lived in hell — a hell of repression lit by flashes of inspiration, when a poem such as this or that would appear

What would have happened in a world similarly lit by the imagination

Oh yes, you are a writter ! a phrase that has often damned me, to myself. I rejected it with heat but the stigma remained. Not a man, not an understanding but a WRITER. I was unable to recognize.

I do not forget with what heat too I condemned some poems of some contemporary praised because of their loveliness —

I find that I was somewhat mistaken — ungenerous

Life's processes are very simple. One or two moves are made and that is the end. The rest is repetitious.

The Improvisations — coming at a time when I was trying to remain firm at great cost — I had recourse to the expedient of letting life go completely in order to live in the world of my choice.

I let the imagination have its own way to see if it could save itself. Something very definite came of it. I found myself alleviated but

most important I began there and then to revalue
experience, to understand what I was at —

The virtue of the improvisations is their placement
in a world of new values —

their fault is their dislocation of
sense, often complete. But it is the best I could do
under the circumstances. It was the best I could
do and retain any value to experience at all.

Now I have come to a different condition. I find
that the values there discovered can be extended. I
find myself extending the understanding to the work
of others and to other things —

I find that there is work to be done in the
creation of new forms, new names for experience

and that « beauty » is related not to « loveliness »
but to a state in which reality playes a part

Such painting as that of Juan Gris, coming after
the impressionists, the expressionists, Cezanne —
and dealing severe strokes as well to the expression-
its as to the impressionists group — points forward
to what will prove the greatest painting yet produced.

— the illusion once dispensed with, painting has

this problem before it : to replace not the forms but
the reality of experience with its own —

up to now shapes and meanings but always the
illusion relying on composition to give likeness to
« nature »

now works of art cannot be left in this category of
France's « lie », they must be real, not « realism » but
reality itself —

they must give not the sense of frustration but a
sense of completion, of actuality — It is not a matter
of « representation » —- much may be represented
actually, but of separate existence.

enlargement — revivification of values,

X

The universality of things
draws me toward the candy
with melon flowers that open

about the edge of refuse
proclaiming without accent
the quality of the farmer's

shoulders and his daughter's
accidental skin, so sweet
with clover and the small

yellow cinquefoil in the
parched places. It is
this that engages the favorable

distortion of eyeglasses
that see everything and remain
related to mathematics —

in the most practical frame of
brown celluloid made to
represent tortoiseshell —

A letter from the man who
wants to start a new magazine
made of linen

and he owns a typewriter —
July 1, 1922
All this is for eyeglasses

to discover. But
they lie there with the gold
earpieces folded down

tranquilly Titicaca —

XI

In passing with my mind
on nothing in the world

but the right of way
I enjoy on the road by

virtue of the law   —
I saw

an elderly man who
smiled and looked away

to the north past a house —
a woman in blue

who was laughing and
leaning forward to look up

into the man's half
averted face

and a boy of eight who was
looking at the middle of

the man's belly
at a watchchain —

The supreme importance
of this nameless spectacle

sped me by them
without a word —

Why bother where I went ?
for I went spinning on the

four wheels of my car
along the wet road until

I saw a girl with one leg
over the rail of a balcony

When in the condition of imaginative suspense
only will the writting have reality, as explained
partially in what preceeds — Not to attempt, at that
time, to set values on the word being used, according
to presupposed measures, but to write down that
which happens at that time —

To perfect the ability to record at the moment
when the consciousness is enlarged by the sympa-
thies and the unity of understanding which the
imagination gives, to practice skill in recording the
force moving, then to know it, in the largeness of
its proportions —-

It is the presence of a

This is not " fit " but a unification of experience

That is, the imagination is an actual force compar-able to electricity or steam, it is not a plaything but a power that has been used from the first to raise the understanding of —· it is, not necessary to resort to mystecisism — In fact it is this which has kept back the knowledge I seek —

The value of the imagination to the writer consists in its ability to make words. Its unique power is to give created forms reality, actual existence

This separates

Writing is not a searching about in the daily experience for apt similies and pretty thoughts and images. I have experienced that to my sorrow. It is not a conscious recording of the day's experiences " freshly and with the appearance of reality " — This sort of thing is seriously to the development of any ability in a man, it fastens him down, makes him a — It destroys, makes nature an accessory to the particular theory he is following, it blinds him to his world, —

The writer of imagination would find himself

released from observing things for the purpose of writing them down later. He would be there to enjoy, to taste, to engage the free world, not a world which he carries like a bag of food, always fearful lest he drop something or someone get more than he,

A world detached from the necessity of recording it, sufficient to itself, removed from him (as it most certainly is) with which he has bitter and delicious relations and from which he is independant — moving at will from one thing to another — as he pleases, unbound — complete

and the unique proof of this is the work of the imagination not " like " anything but transfused with the same forces which transfuse the earth — at least one small part of them.

Nature is the hint to composition not because it is familiar to us and therefore the terms we apply to it have a least common denominator quality which gives them currency — but because it possesses the quality of independant existance, of reality which we feel in ourselves. It is not opposed to art but apposed to it.

I suppose Shakespeare's familiar aphorism about holding the mirror up to nature has done more

harm in stabilizing the copyist tendency of the arts
among us than —

the mistake in it (though we forget that it is not
S. speaking but an imaginative character of his)
is to have believed that the reflection of nature is
nature. It is not. It is only a sham nature, a " lie ".

Of course S. is the most conspicuous example
desirable of the falseness of this very thing.

He holds no mirror up to nature but with his
imagination rivals nature's composition with his
own.

He himself become " nature " — continuing
" its " marvels — if you will

I am often diverted with a recital which I have
made for myself concerning Shakespeare : he was
a comparatively uninformed man, quite according
to the orthodox tradition, who lived from first to
last a life of amusing regularity and simplicity, a
house and wife in the suburbs, delightful children,
a girl at court (whom he really never confused with
his writing) and a café life which gave him with the
freshness of discovery, the information upon which
his imagination fed. London was full of the concen-
trates of science and adventure. He saw at " The

Mermaid " everything he knew. He was not con-
spicuous there except for his spirits.

His form was presented to him by Marlow, his
stories were the common talk of his associates or
else some compiler set them before him. His types
were particularly quickened with life about him.

Feeling the force of life, in his peculiar intelligence,
the great dome of his head, he had no need of any-
thing but writing material to relieve himself of his
thoughts. His very lack of scientific training loosened
his power. He was unencumbered.

For S. to pretend to knowledge would have been
ridiculous — no escape there — but that he possessed
knowledge, and extraordinary knowledge, of the
affairs which concerned him, as they concerned the
others about him, was self-apparent to him. It was
not apparent to the others.

His actual power was PURELY of the imagina-
tion. Not permitted to speak as W.S., in fact pecu-
liarly barred from speaking so because of his lack
of information, learning, not being able to rival his
fellows in scientific training or adventure and at the
same time being keen enough, imaginative enough,
to know that there is no escape except in perfection,
in excellence, in technical excellence — his buoyancy

of imagination raised him NOT TO COPY them, not to holding the mirror up to them but to equal, to surpass them as a creator of knowledge, as a vigorous, living force above their heads.

His escape was not simulated but real. Hamlet no doubt was written about at the middle of his life.

He speaks authoritatively through invention, through characters, through design. The objects of his world were real to him because he could use them and use them with understanding to make his inventions —

The imagination is a —

The vermiculations of modern criticism of S. particularly amuse when the attempt is made to force the role of a Solon upon the creator of Richard 3d.

So I come again to my present day gyrations.

So it is with the other classics : their meaning and worth can only be studied and understood in the imagination — that which begot them only can give them life again, re-enkindle their perfection —

useless to study by rote or scientific research — Useful for certain understanding to corroborate the imagination —

Yes, Anatole was a fool when he said : It is a lie. —
That is it. If the actor simulates life it *is* a lie. But
— but why continue without an audience ?

The reason people marvel at works of art and say :
How in Christ's name did he do it ? — is that they
know nothing of the physiology of the nervous system
and have never in their experience witnessed the
larger processes of the imagination.

It is a step over from the profitless engagements
of the arithmetical.

XII

The red paper box
hinged with cloth

is lined
inside and out
with imitation
leather

It is the sun
the table
with dinner
on it for
these are the same —

Its twoinch trays
have engineers
that convey glue
to airplanes

or for old ladies
that darn socks
paper clips
and red elastics —

What is the end
to insects
that suck gummed
labels ?

for this is eternity
through its
dial we discover
transparent tissue
on a spool

But the stars
are round
cardboard
with a tin edge

and a ring
to fasten them
to a trunk
for the vacation —

XIII

Crustaceous
wedge
of sweaty kitchens
on rock
overtopping
thrusts of the sea

Waves of steel
from
swarming backstreets
shell
of coral
inventing
electricity —

Lights
speckle
El Greco
lakes
in renaissance
twilight
with triphammers

which pulverize
nitrogen

of old pastures
to dodge
motorcars
with arms and legs —

The agregate
is untamed
encapsulating
irritants
but
of agonized spires
knits
peace

where bridge stanchions
rest
certainly
piercing
left ventricles
with long
sunburnt fingers

XIV

Of death
the barber
the barber
talked to me

cutting my
life with
sleep to trim
my hair —

It's just
a moment
he said, we die
every night —

And of
the newest
ways to grow
hair on

bald death —
I told him
of the quartz
lamp

and of old men
with third
sets of teeth
to the cue

of an old man
who said
at the door —
Sunshine today !

for which
death shaves
him twice
a week

XV

The decay of cathedrals
is efflorescent
through the phenomenal
growth of movie houses

whose catholicity is
progress since
destruction and creation
are simultaneous

without sacrifice
of even the smallest
detail even to the
volcanic organ whose

woe is translatable
to joy if light becomes
darkness and darkness
light, as it will —

But scism which seems
adamant is diverted
from thc perpendicular
by simply rotating the object

cleaving away the root of
disaster which it
seemed to foster. Thus
the movies are a moral force

Nightly the crowds
with the closeness and
universality of sand
witness the selfspittle

which used to be drowned
in incense and intoned
over by the supple jointed
imagination of inoffensiveness

backed by biblical
rigidity made into passion plays
upon the altar to
attract the dynamic mob

whose female relative
sweeping grass Tolstoi
saw injected into
the Russian nobility

It is rarely understood how such plays as Shakes-
peare's were written — or in fact how any work of
value has been written, the practical bearing of
which is that only as the work was produced, in that
way alone can it be understood

Fruitless for the academic tapeworm to hoard its
excrementa is books. The cage —

The most of all writing has not even begun in the
province from which alone it can draw sustenance.

There is not life in the stuff because it tries to be
" like " life.

First must come the transposition of the faculties
to the only world of reality that men know : the world
of the imagination, wholly our own. From this
world alone does the work gain power, its soil the
only one whose chemistry is perfect to the purpose.

The exaltation men feel before a work of art
is the feeling of reality they draw from it. It sets
them up, places a value upon experience — (said
that half a dozen times already)

XVI

O tongue
licking
the sore on
her netherlip

O toppled belly

O passionate cotton
stuck with
matted hair

elysian slobber
from her mouth
upon
the folded handkerchief

I can't die

— moaned the old
jaundiced woman
rolling her
saffron eyeballs

I can't die
I can't die

XVII

Our orchestra
is the cat's nuts —

Banjo jazz
with a nickelplated

amplifier to
soothe

the savage beast —
Get the rythm

That sheet stuff
's a lot a cheese.

Man
gimme the key

and lemme loose —
I make 'em crazy

with my harmonies —
Shoot it Jimmy

Nobody
Nobody else

but me —
They can't copy it

XVIII

The pure products of America
go crazy —
mountain folk from Kentucky

or the ribbed north end of
Jersey
with its isolate lakes and

valleys, its deaf-mutes, thieves
old names
and promiscuity between

devil-may-care men who have taken
to railroading
out of sheer lust of adventure —

and young slatterns, bathed
in filth
from Monday to Saturday

to be tricked out that night
with gauds
from imaginations which have no

peasant traditions to give them
character
but flutter and flaunt

sheer rags —- succumbing without
emotion
save numbed terror

under some hedge of choke-cherry
or viburnum —
which they cannot express —

Unless it be that marriage
perhaps
with a dash of Indian blood

will throw up a girl so desolate
so hemmed round
with disease or murder

that she'll be rescued by an
agent —
reared by the state and

sent out at fifteen to work in
some hard pressed
house in the suburbs —

some doctor's family, some Elsie —
voluptuous water
expressing with broken

brain the truth about us —
her great
ungainly hips and flopping breasts

addressed to cheap
jewelry
and rich young men with fine eyes

as if the earth under our feet
were
an excrement of some sky

and we degraded prisoners
destined
to hunger until we eat filth

while the imagination strains
after deer
going by fields of goldenrod in

the stifling heat of September
Somehow
it seems to destroy us

It is only in isolate flecks that
something
is given off

No one
to witness
and adjust, no one to drive the car

   or better : prose has to do with the fact of an
emotion ; poetry has to do with the dynamisation
of emotion into a separate form. This is the force of
imagination.

prose : statement of facts concerning emotions,
intellectua states, data of all sorts — technical expo-
sitions, jargon, of all sorts — fictional and other —

poetry : new form dealt with as a reality in itself.

The form of prose is the accuracy of its subject
matter-how best to expose the multiform phases of
its material

   the form of poetry is related to the movements of
the imagination revealed in words — or whatever
it may be —

the cleavage is complete

Why should I go further than I am able ? Is it not enough for you that I am perfect ?

The cleavage goes through all the phases of experience. It is the jump from prose to the process of imagination that is the next great leap of the intelligence — from the simulations of present experience to the facts of the imagination —

the greatest characteristic of the present age is that it is stale — stale as literature —

To enter a new world, and have there freedom of movement and newness.

I mean that there will always be prose painting, representative work, clever as may be in revealing new phases of emotional research presented on the surface.

But the jump from that to Cezanne or back to certain of the primitives is the impossible.

The primitives are not back in some remote age — they are not BEHIND experience. Work which bridges the gap between the rigidities of vulgar experience and the imagination is rare. It is new, immediate — It is so because it is actual, always real. It is experience dynamized into reality.

Time does not move. Only ignorance and stupidity move. Intelligence (force, power) stands still with time and forces change about itself — sifting the world for permanence, in the drift of nonentity.

Pio Baroja interested me once —

Baroja leaving the medical profession, some not important inspectors work in the north of Spain, opened a bakery in Madrid.

The isolation he speaks of, as a member of the so called intellectual class, influenced him to abandon his position and engage himself, as far as possible, in the intricacies of the design patterned by the social class — He sees no interest in isolation —

These gestures are the effort for self preservation or the preservation of some quality held in high esteem —

Here it seems to be that a man, starved in imagination, changes his milieu so that his food may be richer — The social class, without the power of expression, lives upon imaginative values.

I mean only to emphasize the split that goes down through the abstractions of art to the everyday exercises of the most primitive types —

there is a sharp division — the energizing force of imagination on one side — and the acquisitive — PROGRESSIVE force of the lump on the other

The social class with its religion, its faith, sincerity and all the other imaginative values is positive (yes)

the merchant, hibernating, unmagnatized — tends to drop away into the isolate, inactive particles — Religion is continued then as a form, art as a convention —

To the social, energized class — ebullient now in Russia the particles adhere because of the force of the imagination energizing them —

Anyhow the change of Baroja interested me

Among artists, or as they are sometimes called " men of imagination " " creators ", etc. this force is recognized in a pure state — All this can be used to show the relationships between genius, hand labor, religion — etc. and the lack of feeling between artists and the middle class type —

The jump between fact and the imaginative reality

The study of all human activity is the deliniation of the cresence and ebb of this force, shifting from

class to class and location to location — rhythm : the
wave rhythm of Shakespeare watching clowns and
kings sliding into nothing

XIX

This is the time of year
when boys fifteen and seventeen
wear two horned lilac blossoms
in their caps — or over one ear

What is it that does this ?

It is a certain sort —
drivers for grocers or taxidrivers
white and colored —

fellows that let their hair grow long
in a curve over one eye —

Horned purple

Dirty satyrs, it is
vulgarity raised to the last power

They have stolen them
broken the bushes apart
with a curse for the owner —

Lilacs —

They stand in the doorways
on the business streets with a sneer
on their faces

adorned with blossoms

Out of their sweet heads
dark kisses —- rough faces

XX

The sea that encloses her young body
ula lu la lu
is the sea of many arms —

The blazing secrecy of noon is undone
and and and
the broken sand is the sound of love —

The flesh is firm that turns in the sea
O la la
the sea that is cold with dead mens' tears —

Deeply the wooing that penetrated
to the edge of the sea
returns in the plash of the waves —

a wink over the shoulder
large as the ocean —
with wave following wave to the edge

coom barrooom —

It is the cold of the sea
broken upon the sand by the force
of the moon —

In the sea the young flesh playing
floats with the cries of far off men
who rise in the sea

with green arms
to homage again the fields over there
where the night is deep —

la lu la lu
but lips too few
assume the new — marrruu

Underneath the sea where it is dark
there is no edge
so two —

XXI

one day in Paradise
a Gipsy

smiled
to see the blandness

of the leaves   —
so many

so lascivious
and still

XXII

so much depends
upon

a red wheel
barrow

glazed with rain
water

beside the white
chickens

The fixed categories into which life is divided must always hold. These things are normal — essential to every activity. But they exist — but not as dead dissections.

The curriculum of knowledge cannot but be divided into the sciences, the thousand and one groups of data, scientific, philosophic or whatnot — as many as there exist in Shakespeare — things that make him appear the university of all ages.

But this is not the thing. In the galvanic category of — The same things exist, but in a different condition when energized by the imagination.

The whole field of education is affected — There is no end of detail that is without significance.

Education would begin by placing in the mind of the student the nature of knowledge — in the dead state and the nature of the force which may energize it.

This would clarify his field at once — He would then see the use of data

But at present knowledge is placed before a man as if it were a stair at the top of which a DEGREE is obtained which is superlative.

nothing could be more ridiculous. To data there is no end. There is proficiency in dissection and a knowledge of parts but in the use of knowledge—

It is the imagination that —

That is : life is absolutely simple. In any civilized society everyone should know EVERYTHING there is to know about life at once and always. There should never be permitted, confusion —

There are difficulties to life, under conditions there are impasses, life may prove impossible — But it must never be lost — as it is today —

I remember so distinctly the young Pole in Leipzig going with hushed breath to hear Wundt lecture — In this mass of intricate philosophic data what one of the listeners was able to maintain himself for the winking of an eyelash. Not one. The inundation of the intelligence by masses of complicated fact is not knowledge. There is no end —

And what is the fourth dimension ? It is the end-lessness of knowledge —

It is the imagination on which reality rides — It is the imagination — It is a cleavage through every-thing by a force that does not exist in the mass and therefore can never be discovered by its anatomitization.

It is for this reason that I have always placed art first and esteemed it over science — in spite of everything.

Art is the pure effect of the force upon which science depends for its reality — Poetry

The effect of this realization upon life will be the emplacement of knowledge into a living current — which it has always sought —

In other times — men counted it a tragedy to be dislocated from sense — Today boys are sent with dullest faith to technical schools of all sorts — broken, bruised

few escape whole —slaughter. This is not civilization but stupidity — Before entering knowledge the integrity of the imagination —

The effect will be to give importance to the subdivisions of experience — which today are absolutely lost — There exists simply nothing.

Prose — When values are important, such — For example there is no use denying that prose and poetry are not by any means the same IN INTENTION. But then what is prose ? There is no need for it to approach poetry except to be weakened.

With decent knowledge to hand we can tell what things are for

I except to see values blossom. I expect to see prose be prose. Prose, relieved of extraneous, unrelated values must return to its only purpose : to clarity to enlighten the understanding. There is no form to prose but that which depends on clarity. If prose is not acurately adjusted to the exposition of facts it does not exist — Its form is that alone. To penetrate everywhere with enlightenment —

Poetry is something quite different. Poetry has to do with the crystalization of the imagination — the perfection of new forms as additions to nature — Prose may follow to enlighten but poetry —

Is what I have written prose ? The only answer is that form in prose ends with the end of that which is being communicated — If the power to go on falters in the middle of a sentence — that is the end of the sentence — Or if a new phase enters at that point it is only stupidity to go on.

There is no confusion — only difficulties.

XXIII

The veritable night
of wires and stars

the moon is in
the oak tree's crotch

and sleepers in
the windows cough

athwart the round
and pointed leaves

and insects sting
while on the grass

the whitish moonlight
tearfully

assumes the attitudes
of afternoon —

But it is real
where peaches hang

recalling death's
long promised symphony

whose tuneful wood
and stringish undergrowth

are ghosts existing
without being

save to come with juice
and pulp to assuage

the hungers which
the night reveals

so that now at last
the truth's aglow

with devilish peace
forestalling day

which dawns tomorrow
with dreadful reds

the heart to predicate
with mists that loved

the ocean and the fields —
`Thus moonlight

is the perfect
human touch

XXIV

The leaves embrace
in the trees

it is a wordless
world

without personality
I do not

seek a path
I am still with

Gipsie lips pressed
to my own —

It is the kiss
of leaves

without being
poison ivy

or nettle, the kiss
of oak leaves —

He who has kissed
a leaf

need look no further —-
I ascend

through
a canopy of leaves

and at the same time
I descend

for I do nothing
unusual —

I ride in my car
I think about

prehistoric caves
in the Pyrenees —-

the cave of
Les Trois Freres

The nature of the difference between what is
termed prose on the one hand and verse on the other
is not to be discovered by a study of the metrical
characteristics of the words as they occur in juxta-
position. It is ridiculous to say that verse grades off
into prose as the rythm becomes less and less pro-
nounced, in fact, that verse differs from prose in that
the meter is more pronounced, that the movement is

more impassioned and that rhythmical prose, so called, occupies a middle place between prose and verse.

It is true that verse is likely to be more strongly stressed than what is termed prose, but to say that this is in any way indicative of the difference in nature of the two is surely to make the mistake of arguing from the particular to the general, to the effect that since an object has a certain character that therefore the force which gave it form will always reveal itself in that character.

Of course there is nothing to do but to differentiate prose from verse by the only effective means at hand, the external, surface appearance. But a counter proposal may be made, to wit : that verse is of such a nature that it may appear without metrical stress of any sort and that prose may be strongly stressed — in short that meter has nothing to do with the question whatever.

Of course it may be said that if the difference is felt and is not discoverable to the eye and ear then what about it anyway ? Or it may be argued, that since there is according to my proposal no discoverable difference between prose and verse that in all probability none exists and that both are phases of the same thing.

Yet, quite plainly, there is a very marked differ-
ence between the two which may arise in the
fact of a separate origin for each, each using similar
modes for dis-similar purposes ; verse falling most
commonly into meter but not always, and prose
going forward most often without meter but not
always.

This at least serves to explain some of the best
work I see today and explains some of the most
noteworthy failures which I discover. I search for
" something " in the writing which moves me in a
certain way — It offers a suggestion as to why some
work of Whitman's is bad poetry and some, in the
same meter is prose.

The practical point would be to discover when a
work is to be taken as coming from this source
and when from that. When discovering a work it
would be — If it is poetry it means this and only
this — and if it is prose it means that and only
that. Anything else is a confusion, silly and bad
practice.

I believe this is possible as I believe in the main
that Marianne Moore is of all American writers most
constantly a poet — not because her lines are invar-
iably full of imagery they are not, they are often
diagramatically informative, and not because she

clips her work into certain shapes — her pieces
are without meter most often — but I believe she
is most constantly a poet in her work because
the purpose of her work is invariably from the
source from which poetry starts — that it is con-
stantly from the purpose of poetry. And that it
actually possesses this characteristic, as of that
origin, to a more distinguishable degree when it
eschews verse rhythms than when it does not. It has
the purpose of poetry written into and therefore it
is poetry.

I believe it possible, even essential, that when
poetry fails it does not become prose but bad poetry.
The test of Mariane Moore would be that she writes
sometimes good and sometimes bad poetry but
always — with a single purpose out of a single foun-
tain which is of the sort —

The practical point would be to discover —

I can go no further than to say that poetry feeds
the imagination and prose the emotions, poetry
liberates the words from their emotional implications,
prose confirms them in it. Both move centrifugally
or centripetally toward the intelligence.

Of course it must be understood that writing
deals with words and words only and that all discus-

sions of it deal with single words and their association in groups.

As far as I can discover there is no way but the one I have marked out which will satisfactorily deal with certain lines such as occur in some play of Shakespeare or in a poem of Marianne Moore's, let us say : Tomorrow will be the first of April —

Certainly there is an emotional content in this for anyone living in the northern temperate zone, but whether it is prose or poetry — taken by itself — who is going to say unless some mark is put on it by the intent conveyed by the words which surround it —

Either to write or to comprehend poetry the words must be recognized to be moving in a direction separate from the jostling or lack of it which occurs within the piece.

Marianne's words remain separate, each unwilling to group with the others except as they move in the one direction. This is even an important — or amusing — character of Miss Moore's work.

Her work puzzles me. It is not easy to quote convincingly.

XXV

Somebody dies every four minutes
in New York State —

To hell with you and your poetry —
You will rot and be blown
through the next solar system
with the rest of the gases —

What the hell do you know about it ?

AXIOMS

Do not get killed

Careful Crossing Campaign
Cross Crossings Cautiously

THE HORSES   black
                            &
PRANCED   white

What's the use of sweating over
this sort of thing, Carl ; here
it is all set up —

Outings in New York City

Ho for the open country

Dont't stay shut up in hot rooms
Go to one of the Great Parks
Pelham Bay for example

It's on Long Island Sound
with bathing, boating
tennis, baseball, golf, etc.

Acres and acres of green grass
wonderful shade trees, rippling brooks

      Take the Pelham Bay Park Branch
      of the Lexington Ave. (East Side)
      Line and you are there in a few
      minutes

Interborough Rapid Transit Co.

XXVI

The crowd at the ball game
is moved uniformly

by a spirit of uselessness
which delights them —

all the exciting detail
of the chase

and the escape, the error
the flash of genius —

all to no end save beauty
the eternal —

So in detail they, the crowd,
are beautiful

for this
to be warned against

saluted and defied —
It is alive, venemous

it smiles grimly
its words cut —

The flashy female with her
mother, gets it —

The Jew gets it straight — it
is deadly, terrifying —

It is the Inquisition, the
Revolution

It is beauty itself
that lives

day by day in them
idly —

This is
the power of their faces

It is summer, it is the solstice
the crowd is

cheering, the crowd is laughing
in detail

permanently, seriously
without thought

The imagination uses the phraseology of science. It attacks, stirs, animates, is radio-active in all that can be touched by action. Words occur in liberation by virtue of its processes.

In description words adhere to certain objects. and have the effect on the sense of oysters, or barnacles.

But the imagination is wrongly understood when it is supposed to be a removal from reality in the sense of John of Gaunt's speech in Richard the Second : to imagine possession of that which is lost.

It is rightly understood when John of Gaunt's
words are related not to their sense as objects
adherent to his son's welfare or otherwise but
as a dance over the body of his condition accurately
accompanying it. By this means of the understand-
ing, the play written to be understood as a play,
the author and reader are liberated to pirouette
with the words which have sprung from the old facts
of history, reunited in present passion.

To understand the words as so liberated is to
understand poetry. That they move independantly
when set free is the mark of their value

Imagination is not to avoid reality, nor is it descrip-
tion nor an evocation of objects or situations, it is to
say that poetry does not tamper with the world but
moves it — It affirms reality most powerfully and
therefore, since reality needs no personal support but
exists free from human action, as proven by science
in the indestructibility of matter and of force, it
creates a new object, a play, a dance which is not a
mirror up to nature but —

As birds' wings beat the solid air without which
none could fly so words freed by the imagination
affirm reality by their flight
Writing is likened to music. The object would be
it seems to make poetry a pure art, like music.

Painting too. Writing, as with certain of the modern
Russians whose work I have seen, would use uno-
riented sounds in place of conventional words. The
poem then would be completely liberated when
there is identity of sound with something — perhaps
the emotion.

I do not believe that writing is music. I do not
believe writing would gain in quality or force by
seeking to attain to the conditions of music.

I think the conditions of music are objects for the
action of the writer's imagination just as a table
or —

According to my present theme the writer of
imagination would attain closest to the conditions
of music not when his words are disassociated from
natural objects and specified meanings but when
they are liberated from the usual quality of that
meaning by transposition into another medium,
the imagination.

Sometimes I speak of imagination as a force,
an electricity or a medium, a place. It is immaterial
which : for whether it is the condition of a place or
a dynamization its effect is the same : to free the
world of fact from the impositions of " art " (see
Hartley's last chapter) and to liberate the man to
act in whatever direction his disposition leads.

The word is not liberated, therefore able to communicate release from the fixities which destroy it until it is accurately tuned to the fact which giving it reality, by its own reality establishes its own freedom from the necessity of a word, thus freeing it and dynamizing it at the same time.

XXVII

Black eyed susan
rich orange
round the purple core

the white daisy
is not
enough

Crowds are white
as farmers
who live poorly

But you
are rich
in savagery —

Arab
Indian
dark woman

ERRATA

page 44:	*for* playes	*read* plays
	Cezanne	Cézanne
	expressionits	expressionists
48:	writting	writing
	preceeds	precedes
49:	mystecisism	mysticism
	similies	similes
50:	independant	independent
	"	"
	existance	existence
57:	agregate	aggregate
60:	scism	schism
61:	excrementa is	excrementa in
63:	rythm	rhythm
67:	dynamisation	dynamization
	intellectua	intellectual
	matter-how	matter—how
70:	unmagnatized	unmagnetized
	deliniation	delineation
	cresence	crescence
72:	mens'	men's
77:	anatomitization	anatomization
78:	except	expect
	acurately	accurately
	crystalization	crystallization
81:	Gipsie	Gipsy
82:	*Freres*	*Frères*
82:	rythm	rhythm
84:	diagramatically	diagrammatically
85:	Mariane	Marianne
88:	Dont't	Don't
89	venemous	venomous
90	objects.	objects,
91:	independantly	independently